Does an Apple a Day Keep the Doctor Away?

And Other Questions about Your Health and Body

SANDY DONOVAN

ILLUSTRATIONS BY COLIN W. THOMPSON

LERNER PUBLICATIONS COMPANY

Minneapolis

Contents

Perhaps you've heard these common sayings about your health and body:

An apple a day
keeps the doctor away!
If you cross your eyes,
they might stay that way!

But are these sayings true?
Is there any science behind the stories?
Come along with us as we explore
these old beliefs and more. Find out whether
the stories and sayings you've
heard about your health and body are

FACT OR FICTION!

Can You Catch a Cold If You Go Outside with Wet Hair?

NOPE. Going outside with wet hair may give you a big headache. (Some people call this a brain-freeze headache.) But it won't give you a cold.

A cold is a virus. Cold viruses travel through the air in invisible droplets. When they get inside your body, your immune system kicks in to fight them. This leads to a stuffy nose, sore throat, and headache—in other words, a cold. You have to come in contact with the cold virus to get a cold. And the cold virus has to come from someone who has a cold. The virus travels from a cold sufferer's body to the rest of the world through sneezing, coughing, and touching. And the virus can live for three hours as it travels around invisibly. So being around someone who has a cold can definitely cause a cold.

Bodies are also more likely to get a cold when they are run down. People who don't get enough sleep or don't eat healthfully are more likely to get colds. And, if your body becomes extra chilled—say, from being outside with wet hair—it may get extra tired. That's because it uses up energy shivering. That extra tiredness can make it more likely that it will get sick. So, while being outside with wet hair won't cause a cold, it may make it more likely that you'll get sick if you come in contact with the cold virus.

Do Humans Really Use Only 10 Percent of Their Brains?

ABSOLUTELY NOT!

People have been repeating this myth for decades. Psychics—people who say they can tell what others are thinking or predict the future—often repeat it. They say that people can learn to use the "unused" 90 percent of their brain for psychic activities. But it's not true. All of us use almost all of our brain, every single day.

The brain is more complicated than any computer. It receives messages about everything your body does—seeing, hearing, tasting, smelling, and touching. Then it sorts out this information by doing some heavy work. It remembers things, compares them, and sorts them. It solves problems you didn't even know you had. It also figures out what the other parts of your body should do in any situation.

The brain has three main parts. The outside layer is the cerebrum. It has different areas that receive different kinds of messages. One area gets all the messages about hearing. Another gets all the messages about touch. The cerebellum is a smaller brain part. It sits at the bottom of the brain. It's in charge of coordinating muscles. The third brain part is the brain stem. This tube is in charge of keeping automatic body systems working. It keeps your heart beating so you don't have to think about it.

Did You Know?

Your brain grows until you are about twenty years old. But it can keep on learning new things long after that. In fact, your brain never really stops learning. It can make new connections until you are at least one hundred!

It seems as if it would be hard to do all these things with only 10 percent of a brain, doesn't it? And indeed, doctors can *prove* that we use all of our brains. They use PET scans to look at the brain. *PET* stands for positron-emission tomography. This technology lets doctors see what's going on inside the body. With PET scans, doctors have seen that all areas of the brain are used.

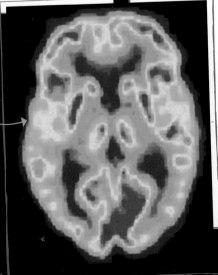

PET scans—such as this one—show that humans use all areas of the brain.

Can You Harm Your Eyes by Reading in the Dark?

NO. Reading in the dark can make your eyes tired. But it won't cause permanent damage. In fact, very few things can actually harm your eyes. You may have been warned about lots of things that can supposedly hurt your vision. Don't watch too much TV. Don't work at a computer for too long. Don't read too small print. **None of these activities can harm your eyes for good. But they can all cause eyestrain.**

Eyestrain is a type of muscle strain. Muscle strain can happen when you work a muscle very hard. You may get strained leg muscles after a long run. And you may get strained eye muscles after making an effort to read in the dark.

Reading in dim light or doing lots of close-up work can bring on eyestrain.

When you have eyestrain, your eyes will feel tired. The muscles circling your eyes may ache. Eyestrain can lead to a headache. It can also cause watery or dry eyes. If you feel these symptoms, it's a sign that you should take a break from whatever you are doing. If you're reading in a room with dim lights, turn on a lamp. For reading in bed, try a small light with an adjustable neck. This lets you shine light right where you need it. If you're concentrating really hard on close-up work, give your eye muscles a rest. Try closing your eyes for a minute. Or try staring off into the distance for a while.

Of course, if you seem to experience eyestrain a lot, you should tell a doctor. Sometimes eyestrain can be a sign of a more serious eye condition.

Take Good Care of Your Eyes

Too much TV watching won't harm your eyes. But too much sun will. Remember to wear sunglasses or a wide-brimmed hat to protect your eyes in the sun.

Can Eating Junk Food Give You Acne?

It's never a good idea to eat too much junk food. **BUT EATING POORLY DOESN'T CAUSE ACNE.**

Acne is an outbreak of blackheads or whiteheads. Blackheads and whiteheads are kinds of pimples. They form when the body's natural oils get trapped inside the skin's pores (small openings where hair grows through the skin).

Pores connect to oil glands. Oil glands lie deep beneath the skin's surface. They produce an oil called sebum. Sebum travels through the pores and ends up on the skin. There it forms a waterproof barrier for the body. It keeps the skin nice and smooth. As an added bonus, it also keeps dirt off pores. But if the sebum gets trapped inside the pores, bacteria can build up. Then the pores can get clogged. That's when a whitehead or blackhead appears.

Whiteheads occur when a pore becomes completely clogged. Then it closes up. The sebum and bacteria collect in the pore and form a small white bump. Blackheads develop when a pore clogs but doesn't close up. The sebum in the pore turns black when it mixes with the outside air. This leaves a tiny black spot on the pore.

Did You Know?

Scientists say that eight out of ten preteens and teens get acne at some point.

So why do some people get blackheads and whiteheads while others don't? Unfortunately, this has to do with a kind of science you can't do anything about. It's called genetics. It's all about the traits passed down from parents to kids. This means if your birth parents had pimples as teens, chances are that you will too.

Do Carrots Improve Your Vision?

Eating carrots won't make you see better. But as the spokesperson for the American Academy of Ophthalmology (eye medicine) says, "You never see any rabbits wearing glasses!"

IT'S TRUE THAT CARROTS ARE GOOD FOR YOUR EYES. They contain beta-carotene. Beta-carotene becomes vitamin A when the body breaks it down. And the body needs vitamin A to maintain normal vision.

What *isn't* true is that eating foods with vitamin A will make your vision stronger. Most people in developed countries get enough vitamin A as part of their regular diets. Extra vitamin A won't give their eyes any extra power. But in countries with shortages of healthful foods, many people suffer from a lack of vitamin A. They may even experience blindness because of the vitamin A shortage. In this instance, eating carrots could definitely help improve vision.

Even though carrots won't make your vision better, it's still important to get plenty of vitamin A. In addition to carrots, you can eat eggs and drink milk to get your daily dose. Remember: a balanced diet with a variety of vitamins will keep your eyes—as well as the rest of your body—healthy and strong.

Turning Orange

Eating lots of carrots may not give you superpowered eyes. But it can have one interesting effect. It can make your skin turn orange! That's right. If you eat more than three large carrots a day, you may start to notice an orange glow—especially on the soles of your feet and the palms of your hands. But don't worry. It's nothing serious. And it isn't permanent! So keep on eating all the carrots you want.

Can Eating Chicken Soup Cure a Cold?

For centuries, mothers have been cooking chicken soup whenever their children have come down with colds. Even doctors have recommended chicken soup to patients with colds. But does this old remedy really work? Or does it just make you feel a little better while you're eating it?

Most people agree that warm soup can feel good on a sore throat. And soup's steam may help unclog a stuffy nose. But couldn't any hot drink—tea, cider, or even cocoa—do that? **ACTUALLY, SOME SCIENTISTS SAY THE INGREDIENTS IN CHICKEN SOUP MAKE IT GOOD MEDICINE.**

Here's why. A cold is caused by a virus in the nose, throat, or chest. Special white blood cells rush around those areas attacking the virus. These cells are called neutrophils. But while neutrophils are rushing around fighting the virus, they're also doing something else. All their rushing makes mucus grow. Mucus is the stuff that clogs your nose during a cold.

Believe it or not, it's a good sign if your nose stuffs up when you're sick. It means your white blood cells are doing their job.

A scientist at the University of Nebraska wanted to see if chicken soup had any effect on neutrophils. He added some chicken soup to the white blood cells. He found that the soup actually slowed down the movement of the cells. This in turn slowed down the growth of mucus. There it was: scientific evidence that chicken soup could slow down cold symptoms.

So what exactly is in chicken soup that helps it fight a cold? The scientist couldn't tell. But he guessed it might be a combination of ingredients: the veggies, the fat from the chicken, and even the salt. Scientists need to do more research to answer that question. Meanwhile, next time you feel a cold coming on, reach for some chicken soup!

Should You Really Wait a Half Hour after Eating before You Swim?

NO NEED. For years kids have been hearing about the dangers of swimming with a full stomach. But it turns out there's really very little danger.

It's usually parents and grandparents who describe how swimming after eating can lead to a stomach cramp. Then, they say, you'll be in so much pain, you won't be able to make your way out of the water. Another version of the warning says your body sends all its oxygen to your stomach after you eat, to help with digestion. This leaves too little oxygen for your muscles to work. So you can't swim, and you drown.

In fact, these warnings do have some truth. You *can* develop a cramp while swimming with a full stomach. When your stomach is full, your stomach muscles are working to digest. Muscles work by contracting (squeezing together) and then relaxing. But if you're swimming or doing other exercise, your stomach muscles might not be able to relax right away. This can cause a cramp. But while the pain may be annoying, it won't keep you from making your way out of the water.

It's also true that the body sends oxygen to the stomach after eating. Arm and leg muscles need oxygen to work. But it's *not* true that arm and leg muscles wouldn't get enough oxygen because it was all going to the stomach. The body uses blood to carry oxygen to its different parts. And it has plenty of blood to supply oxygen to the stomach and the arms and legs at the same time.

Swimming after eating can cause a cramp—but it isn't deadly!

So diving in for a swim right after eating won't kill you. But it might cause a little pain. If you feel too full after eating, rest for a while. After a few minutes, you'll probably feel up to a swim.

Is Yawning Contagious?

YES, IT IS! Most scientists agree that there is something catching about seeing someone else yawn. It almost always causes people who see the yawn to yawn themselves. Scientists have even done yawning studies on other animals. In one study, they showed videos of yawning chimpanzees to other chimpanzees. Without fail, the chimps watching the videos started yawning away.

Humans aren't the only ones who can catch a case of the yawns. Yawning is contagious for chimps and other animals too.

A yawn is just a simple act of taking extra air into the lungs. First, the mouth opens. Then the yawner inhales and takes in enough air to fill the lungs. Finally, the extra air is released back through the mouth.

So scientists are still trying to figure out exactly why we yawn. When they know that,

But no one knows why yawning is contagious. In fact, scientists can't even agree on why the human body yawns. They are pretty sure that yawning is involuntary (done without choice). For many years, people thought yawns were the body's way of getting enough oxygen. When people are tired, they breathe more slowly. As a result, they take in less oxygen. One big yawn can make up for that. It draws in plenty of good oxygen and lets out bad carbon dioxide (a gas that all animals exhale). But lately, some experiments have shown that bodies with low rates of oxygen do not, in fact, yawn more.

perhaps they'll uncover why yawning is contagious as well. Meanwhile, try this experiment: The next time you're sitting with a group of people—not in class, please; you need to concentrate in class—let out a big yawn. Then watch to see how long it takes for others in the group to start yawning.

Did You Know?

Even reading about yawning is contagious. See if reading these pages about yawning makes you yawn.

When You Drop Food on the Floor, Is It Safe to Eat It If You Pick It Up In Five Seconds?

You've probably heard of the "five-second rule." It says that germs from the floor won't transfer to food as long as you pick it up in five seconds. **UNFORTUNATELY, THE FIVE-SECOND RULE IS A MYTH.** No matter how delicious-looking that bite of food was, once it hits the floor, it's covered in whatever germs lie there.

All kinds of germs live on floors. They travel on the bottom of shoes and drift down through the air. Most germs are either viruses or bacteria. Both of these kinds of germs can make you sick. Kitchen floors are often contaminated with bacteria from meat that hasn't been cooked. Germs from bathrooms are easily tracked on shoes throughout houses. And every time someone sneezes, any virus the person may be carrying is sure to end up on the floor.

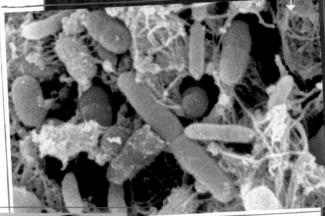

These bacteria are from uncooked chicken meat. Such bacteria often live on kitchen floors.

In 2003 a high school student named Jillian Clarke did a study of the five-second rule. She sprayed a floor with *E. coli* (a bacterium that can be harmful to humans). Then she dropped gummy bears and cookies on the floor. Finally, she examined the candy and cookies under a microscope. She found that even before five seconds had passed, the candy and the cookies had picked up enough bacteria to make a person sick.

Jillian Clarke

Unfortunately, it's almost impossible to know if a floor is germy or not. Even the cleanest-looking floor can be covered with germs. So the best rule to follow is to not eat *any* food that has fallen on the floor. And if something like a fork or a baby's pacifier drops on a floor, wash it off with hot, soapy water. Running something under tap water will not remove germs.

Do We Really Need to Drink Eight Glasses of Water a Day?

NO! For many years, magazine articles on health and nutrition have been telling people about the benefits of drinking plenty of water. The most common advice is to drink at least eight 8-ounce (0.2-liter) glasses of water each day. According to the advice, drinking enough water can help people feel less tired, lose weight, and even avoid getting cancer. But are these claims true?

In 2002 a professor from Dartmouth Medical School decided to try to track down any evidence to support the eight-glasses-of-water-a-day advice. He read through all the research on water drinking. And he found that there was no evidence that people actually need that much water.

In fact, the human body needs to take in as much fluid as it excretes—or gets rid of—each day. Some experiments have shown that bodies excrete up to 10 cups (2.3 liters) of water a day. But they probably take in as much as 5 cups (1 liter) just through regular eating. That's because common foods such as fruits, veggies, and prepared soups all contain fluid. So that leaves about 5 cups of fluid per day that a body needs to replace. And all of that replacement fluid does not have to be water. It can be milk, juice, or—according to some doctors—even soda.

Fruits and veggies contain plenty of water.

So don't worry about counting glasses of water throughout the day. Instead, eat a healthful diet that includes plenty of fruits and veggies. And drink when you are thirsty.

Health Tip
Water does not have to be your only source of fluid, but it is one of the most healthful drinks around. It contains none of the sugar or caffeine found in many prepared drinks.

Can You Cure Nighttime Leg Cramps by Sleeping with a Bar of Soap?

UNDETERMINED. Believe it or not, nobody has been able to disprove this claim. And lots of people say it works.

If you've ever woken up in the middle of the night with an intense leg cramp, you know how desperate people can get to avoid these painful incidents. Leg cramps usually happen in the calf muscle. The calf muscle involuntarily tightens. Muscles often tighten and then release. But during a cramp, the muscle doesn't release. This causes pain that's severe enough to wake up even a heavy sleeper.

Lots of people have spent lots of time trying to figure out how to avoid nighttime leg cramps. One of the things that seems to work is sleeping with a bar of soap under the sheets. Many people have reported that this has cured their leg cramps. It doesn't seem to matter if the soap is wrapped, unwrapped, placed under the calf, or just tucked into the bed somewhere. Scientists have not been able to figure out why the soap might prevent cramps. Some think one of the soap's ingredients may help relax muscles. Others think this remedy works because people want it to work. That is, they think the success is in people's heads. Whatever the reason, hundreds of people claim to have ended their nighttime cramps thanks to placing soap under the sheets.

Could plain old bars of soap be a cure for nighttime leg cramps? Lots of people say yes!

SOAP

Does an Apple a Day Keep the Doctor Away?

UNFORTUNATELY, THERE'S NO SURE WAY TO AVOID GETTING SICK OR NEEDING A DOCTOR.

But eating fruit and veggies can certainly help keep you healthy. That's where this saying comes from. Nobody's sure who first said this line, but it probably wasn't meant to be taken word for word. Instead, "an apple a day" probably means a person should eat fruit every day. And "keep the doctor away" probably means staying healthy—not actually keeping all doctors away from you.

There's a lot of truth to this saying. People definitely need to eat fruit and veggies to stay healthy. Doctors recommend eating at least five servings of fruits and veggies each day. And it's important to mix up the fruits and veggies you eat. That way you get a wider variety of vitamins and nutrients (healthful substances found in food).

In looking for a variety of fruits and veggies, think color. Orange and dark green veggies, for example, each provide different nutrients. To find out exactly how many servings of fruits and veggies you need, visit http://www.fruitsandveggiesmatter.gov.

Red and green apples contain different nutrients than orange tangerines or yellow bananas—so eat all kinds of fruits and veggies to stay healthy!

Can Listening to Loud Music Cause Hearing Loss?

YES, IT CAN! So turn that music down. And be sure to avoid too much exposure to other really loud sounds too.

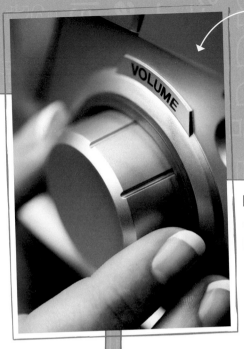

Keep the volume down to help protect your ears!

The vibrations—or small, shaking movements—caused by loud sounds are what lead to hearing loss. Here's how it happens:

The ear has three areas—the outer, middle, and inner ear. The outer ear is the part you can see. Sound vibrations move into the ear through the outer ear. Soon they hit the eardrum. The eardrum separates the outer ear and middle ear. When sound vibrations hit the eardrum, it vibrates. This movement then causes three small bones in the middle ear to vibrate. This, in turn, leads to movement inside the inner ear. Tiny hairs in the inner ear pick up the movement. They turn the movement into nerve impulses that are sent to the brain. The brain understands this as sound.

Loud noises can damage the tiny hairs of the inner ear. The vibrations caused by loud sounds can knock down the hairs. Often, the hairs can recover. Then normal hearing returns. But sometimes the hairs actually break. If the hairs are broken, they can never grow back. Then the hearing damage is permanent. This is why it's important for people who are around loud noise a lot to wear ear protection. Professional musicians, construction workers, and airport workers often wear earplugs on the job.

Listening to music on earbuds can be particularly harmful to ears. But turning it down just a little can help prevent hearing loss. Doctors estimate that people can safely listen to iPods at 90 percent volume for only five minutes a day. But by turning the volume down to 70 percent, they can safely listen for 4.6 hours per day.

Did You Know?

Tinnitus, or ringing in the ears, is a common side effect of noise-related hearing damage.

Can You Hurt Your Knuckles If You Crack Them Too Much?

POSSIBLY. Some people say that knuckle cracking can cause arthritis. (Arthritis is a condition that makes people's joints swell up and hurt.) This isn't true. Genetics or past joint injuries cause most arthritis cases. Knuckle cracking has nothing to do with it. What knuckle cracking can do is irritate the tendons (thick bands of tissue that join muscles to bones). It can also lead to swelling in the hands. So it's a good idea to keep knuckle popping to a minimum.

It might sound as if your bones are cracking against one another when you pop your knuckles. But it's really only gas inside your joints that's making that sound. The gas is called synovial fluid. This liquid keeps your joints moving well. When you tug on a finger to crack your knuckle, you create a bubble in the synovial fluid. With continued stretching, the bubble pops open. That's what makes the cracking sound you hear when you pop your knuckles.

Immediately after you crack your knuckles, your joints might feel loose. You may actually be able to move them more than usual. But this feeling does not last long. When you pop open the bubbles in synovial fluid, you are also stretching your tendons over bony parts of your hand. And scientists say that doing this a lot can damage the tendons and make your hands swell over time.

Did You Know?

Repeated knuckle cracking is similar to the repeated movements of professional baseball pitchers. After years of pitching, many pitchers suffer from damaged shoulder joints.

31

If You Cross Your Eyes, Will They Stay That Way?

Crossing your eyes on purpose may tire your eye muscles. But it won't lead to permanently crossed eyes.

In fact, while nearly every child has crossed his or her eyes on purpose at least once, only about 4 percent of children in the United States have cross-eye. This condition's real name is strabismus. Strabismus causes the eyes to line up incorrectly. It makes a person's eyes appear as if they are looking in two different directions.

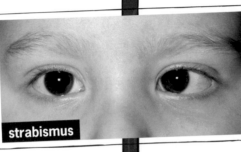

strabismus

When strabismus causes the eyes to turn outward, it's sometimes called walleye. When it causes the eyes to turn inward, it's often called cross-eye. Either way, strabismus interferes with normal vision. It makes focusing on an object very difficult.

The reason focusing is hard for people with strabismus is that each of their eyes sends a different picture to their brain. As a result, their brain receives either a double image or a blurry image. To try to correct the problem, the brain often shuts off the images it gets from one of the eyes. This helps the brain get a clear image—but it also makes one eye get weak. This can lead to another eye condition called lazy eye, or amblyopia.

Strabismus and amblyopia are both often treated with prescription glasses. Glasses can help the eyes focus in the correct manner. Kids with amblyopia may also wear an eye patch to help strengthen their weak eye.

As for crossing your eyes on purpose—doctors probably won't recommend that you do it all the time. But it's not going to cause either strabismus or amblyopia.

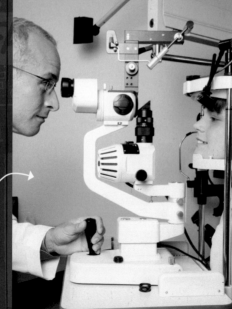

Getting regular eye exams can help protect your eyes and keep them healthy.

Can Eating Fish Make You Smarter?

ACCORDING TO SOME SCIENTISTS, THE ANSWER IS YES. Research has already shown that fish is great for the body. It contains protein and vitamins A and D. We need these nutrients to grow and maintain strength. But lately, scientists have been finding more and more evidence that fish is good for the mind as well. Specifically, the oils found in fish are thought to help the brain. These oils contain omega-3 fatty acids. These special fats have been shown to improve brain development in babies born to mothers who ate enough of them.

New studies have also shown that omega-3 fatty acids can help older people keep their minds sharp. In one study, more than two thousand older adults kept track of how much omega-3-rich fish they ate each day. Then they took tests of their brainpower. The people who ate at least 3 ounces (85 grams) of fish a day scored higher on the tests than people who ate less fish. Other studies have shown similar results.

The studies aren't enough to absolutely prove that eating fish can make you smarter. But it may still be worth a try. Even if it doesn't make you smarter, fish is a healthful food that provides nutrients your body needs.

If you don't like fish, you can also find omega-3 fatty acids in other foods, including flax seeds and flax seed oil (above), walnuts, kiwifruit, leafy greens, and eggs.

BRAIN
POWER
TEST
IN
PROGRESS

Does Eating Spinach Give You Big Muscles?

NOT BY ITSELF. But the belief that spinach can give you big muscles is so popular that it even has its own name: the Popeye effect. It's named after the cartoon character Popeye *(right)*. You've probably seen this guy with the sailor suit and huge biceps. He's known for popping open cans of spinach with his bare hands. The implication is that all that spinach gave him supersized muscles.

Spinach is a powerful food, but spinach alone won't give you muscles like Popeye's. To get large muscles, you need a variety of foods and regular exercise. However, spinach is packed with iron and magnesium. These nutrients help bring oxygen from the lungs to the muscles. And muscles need oxygen to grow.

One trick to getting the most out of the nutrients in spinach is to eat it along with a dairy product. (Milk, cheese, and yogurt are a few.) Dairy products contain calcium. Calcium helps the body break down and absorb iron. So the next time you have a spinach salad, some steamed spinach, or a spinach stir-fry, follow it up with a serving of your favorite dairy treat. You may not get muscles like Popeye right away. But you'll be on your way!

Spinach is packed with nutrients that help your muscles grow. Exercise those muscles to get even stronger!

Oops!

The rumor that spinach builds big muscles began more than one hundred years ago. In 1870 a scientist recording the nutritional content of vegetables accidentally misplaced a decimal point. His records mistakenly showed that spinach had ten times more iron than any other green vegetable. It was sixty-seven years before the mistake was corrected. But by then, the Popeye cartoon had already been around for eight years—and many people believed in the Popeye effect.

SPINACH
10 X
MORE
IRON
than

GLOSSARY

acne: an outbreak of pimples on the skin

amblyopia: an eye disorder in which one eye is weaker than the other. Amblyopia is also called lazy eye.

arthritis: a condition that makes people's joints swell up and hurt

bacteria: microscopic living things that exist all around you and inside you

beta-carotene: a nutrient found in carrots and many other dark orange and green vegetables and fruits. Beta-carotene becomes vitamin A when the body breaks it down.

bicep: a large muscle on the front of your arm between your shoulder and inner elbow

brain stem: the part of the brain that keeps the automatic body systems working. The brain stem controls things such as the heartbeat, digestion, and breathing.

carbon dioxide: a gas that all animals exhale

cerebellum: the part of the brain that is in charge of coordinating muscles. The cerebellum sits at the bottom of the brain.

cerebrum: the outside layer of the brain. The cerebrum has different areas that receive messages about different things, such as hearing and touch.

excrete: to pass waste matter out of the body

eyestrain: a type of muscle strain that can happen when you work your eyes very hard. Eyestrain can occur when you read in poor light or do a lot of close-up work.

immune system: the system that protects your body against disease and infection

involuntary: done without choice

neutrophil: a special type of white blood cell that attacks viruses in the body

nutrient: a healthful substance found in food

omega-3 fatty acids: special fats found in fish oil. Omega-3 fatty acids have been shown to improve brain function.

pore: a small opening where hair grows through the skin

psychic: a person who claims to be able to tell what others are thinking or to predict the future

sebum: an oil produced by oil glands that lie beneath the skin's surface

strabismus: an eye disorder that causes the eyes to line up incorrectly

synovial fluid: a gas inside your joints. Synovial fluid keeps your joints moving well.

tendon: a thick band of tissue that joins a muscle to a bone or another body part

tinnitus: ringing in the ears. Tinnitus is a common side effect of noise-related hearing damage.

virus: a very tiny organism that can reproduce and grow only when inside living cells. Viruses cause illnesses such as colds.

SOURCE NOTE

12 Jessica Cohn, "Seeing and Believing: Take a Long Look at Eye-Health Myths," *Current Health* no. 3 (October 1, 2007): page 20.

SELECTED BIBLIOGRAPHY

Fox, Stuart Ira. *Human Physiology.* 10th ed. New York: McGraw-Hill, 2007.

Government of South Australia. "The Brain." *Children, Youth, and Women's Health Service: Kids Health.* May 11, 2007. http://www.cyh.com/ HealthTopics/HealthTopicDetailsKids .aspx?p=335&np=152&id=1528 (December 31, 2007).

Nemours Foundation. *KidsHealth.* N.d. http://www.kidshealth.org (December 31, 2007).

University of Illinois Eye & Ear Infirmary. "Vision Myths." *Eye Digest.* June 17, 2007. http://www.agingeye.net/vision-basics/visionmyths.php (December 31, 2007).

Urban Legends Reference Pages. *Snopes .com.* N.d. http://www.snopes.com (December 31, 2007).

FURTHER READING

Avison, Brigid. *I Wonder Why I Blink: And Other Questions about My Body.* New York: Kingfisher Books, 1993. Learn more about your health and body in this easy-to-read book. It explores questions such as What are goose bumps? Why do I get hiccups? Why can't I see in the dark?

BAM! Body and Mind
http://www.bam.gov
Visit this website to get the real scoop on topics related to your health and body.

Doeden, Matt. *Stay Fit!: How You Can Get in Shape.* Minneapolis: Lerner Publications Company, 2009. Doeden reveals the truth about how to maintain your body's health and fitness.

Everyday Mysteries
http://www.loc.gov/rr/scitech/mysteries
Check out this site to find the answers to some interesting questions about food, nutrition, the body, and more.

Kallen, Stuart A. *Urban Legends.* Farmington Hills, MI: Lucent Books, 2006. This in-depth book contains a wealth of information on urban legends—those well-known myths and stories about health, food, animals, celebrities, and other topics.

KidsHealth
http://kidshealth.org/kid
This site has the answers to lots of common questions about health.

Packard, Mary. *Mythbusters: Don't Try This at Home!* San Francisco: Jossey-Bass, 2006. Come along with Adam Savage and Jamie Hyneman—stars of the popular Discovery Channel show *Mythbusters*—as they examine fifteen fascinating myths.

INDEX

ACKNOWLEDGMENTS

The images in this book are used with the permission of:
© iStockphoto.com/Sandy Jones, pp. 1, 4 (right), 27 (inset); © Scientifica/ADEAR/Visuals Unlimited, Inc., pp. 2 (left), 7 (bottom); © iStockphoto.com/Gaby Jalbert, pp. 2 (top right), 12 (inset); © Art Wolfe/Stone/Getty Images, pp. 2 (bottom right), 19 (bottom); © iStockphoto.com/Paul W. Brain, pp. 3 (top), 4 (left); © Jose Luis Pelaez Inc./Blend Images/Getty Images, pp. 3 (bottom), 32; © Glow Images, Inc./SuperStock, p. 5; © Anatomical Travelogue/Photo Researchers, Inc., p. 6; © Alex Mares-Manton/Asia Images/Getty Images, p. 7 (top); © Philip Condit II/Riser/Getty Images, pp. 8–9; © Michael Goldman/The Image Bank/Getty Images, p. 9 (top); © iStockphoto.com/foto-bacca, p. 9 (bottom); © iStockphoto.com/Ermin Gutenberger, p. 10 (background); © Lisa Pines/Taxi/Getty Images, p. 10 (inset); © PHANIE/Photo Researchers, Inc., p. 11; © iStockphoto.com/ Marie Fields, pp. 12–13; © Mediscan/Visuals Unlimited, Inc., p. 13 (inset); © Ron Chapple Studios/Dreamstime.com, pp. 14–15; © iStockphoto.com/Kathy Burns-Millyard, p. 15; © Andersen Ross/Iconica/Getty Images, pp. 16-17; © iStockphoto.com/Galina Barskaya, p. 17 (inset); © Steve Prezant/CORBIS, p. 18; © Arco Images GmbH/Alamy, p. 19 (top); © Stock4B/Getty Images, p. 20; © Simko/Visuals Unlimited, Inc., p. 21 (top); Courtesy of Jillian Clarke, p. 21 (bottom); © iStockphoto.com/Susan Trigg, pp. 22–23; © iStockphoto. com/Jack Puccio, p. 23 (inset); © mediablitzimages (uk) Limited/Alamy, p. 24; © Todd Strand/Independent Picture Service, p. 25 (both); © age fotostock/SuperStock, pp. 26–27; © Somos/Veer/Getty Images, pp. 28–29; © Jeffrey Coolidge/The Image Bank/Getty Images, p. 29; © Dr. Barry Slaven/Visuals Unlimited, Inc., pp. 30–31; © Doug Benc/Getty Images, p. 31 (inset); © Dr P. Marazzi/Photo Researchers, Inc., p. 33 (top); © UpperCut Images/Getty Images, p. 33 (bottom); © iStockphoto.com/Brigitte Smith, pp. 34–35; © Envision/CORBIS, p. 35 (inset); © Image Source/Getty Images, p. 36 (background); Everett Collection, p. 36 (inset); © Tanya Constantine/Photodisc/Getty Images, p. 37.

Front Cover: © iStockphoto.com/Paul W. Brain (left); © iStockphoto.com/Sean Locke (right).

Lerner Publications Company
A division of Lerner Publishing Group, Inc.
241 First Avenue North
Minneapolis, MN 55401 U.S.A.

Website address: www.lernerbooks.com

Library of Congress Cataloging-in-Publication Data

Donovan, Sandra, 1967–
    Does an apple a day keep the doctor away? : and other questions about your health and body / by Sandy Donovan; illustrated by Colin W. Thompson.
        p.   cm. — (Is that a fact?)
    Includes bibliographical references and index.
    ISBN 978-0-8225-9084-2 (lib. bdg. : alk. paper)
    1. Health—Miscellanea. I. Thompson, Colin W., ill. II. Title.
RA776.D675 2010
610—dc22   2009010223

Manufactured in the United States of America
1 – JR – 12/15/2009